Gander

The Town That Welcomed the World

Thank you, Gander. Through your kindness,
you left a heart print in the lives of many.
—Nikki

For my family, and anyone who helps
those in need.
—Reilly

Gander

The Town That Welcomed the World

By Nikki Bergstresser
Art by Reilly Fitzgerald

PLUMLEAF PRESS

Like geese flying over on an autumn day, the planes came to the small Canadian town of Gander.

One by one, they landed on the tarmac.

The skies grew silent. Air travel around the world came to a sudden stop.

FLYING

More than 6,000 people on 38 planes arrived.
An unplanned stop on their journey.

Minutes then hours went by.

Sitting.

Waiting.

News buzzed around the town. Questions filled the air about the "plane people."

Did you hear?

Do you know how many people?

How can we help?

What happens next?

Word spread faster than a fiddler's jig.

No one knew how long the unexpected visitors would be stranded in Gander. It was time to put a plan into action.

The people of Gander collected sleeping bags, pillows, towels, and even toys from every closet in every house.

They gathered groceries and made meals.

Everything was delivered to the locations where the guests would be housed.

Welcome mats were laid out.

Even the bus drivers of Gander, who had been on strike, laid down their picket signs to help.

Many of the passengers, who were from around the world, had never heard of Newfoundland, or this town called Gander.

Sitting.

Waiting.

With each hour spent in the crowded planes, their worry grew.

GA

Finally, permission was granted for everyone to deplane and step onto Canadian soil. Some passengers had been waiting more than twenty-four hours for this news.

People of all ages began to walk down the steps of the planes.

Tired and hungry.

Confused.

But a surprise was waiting for them.

MONTREAL
NEW YORK
GANDER
WELCOME

Walking through the terminal doors, the weary plane people were met with a sea of smiling faces, ready to help. Sandwiches had been made throughout the night for all who were hungry.

A world map hung on the wall with an arrow pointing to Gander and the words printed

"YOU ARE HERE."

Buses full of passengers arrived at the schools, churches, community halls, and homes in Gander and other neighbouring towns.

The guests made calls to loved ones across the world to let them know they were safe.

The Newfoundlanders and their guests exchanged names, stories, and music while sharing hearty meals of casseroles, stews, and cakes.

Luggage was not allowed to come off the planes. Any items the passengers needed, they were given. Medicine, toothbrushes, socks, and even clean underwear were provided.

So much toilet paper was donated that an announcement was sent out:

“Hold the TP!”

The visitors rested in beds and cots, warmed with donated blankets.

BREAD
MEAT

The people of Gander turned the local hockey rink into a refrigerator to store the donated food from surrounding communities.

Animal shelter volunteers were given time to search through cargo areas of the planes for any animals on board.

They took the dogs, cats, and a pair of bonobos named Unga and Kosana to a safe place to stay with food and care.

For six days, the people of Gander gave.

But it wasn't all work. Time for play was important too.

Hosts took their guests on sightseeing trips, moose spotting, and berry picking.

There was something for everyone, including boat rides, toe-tapping music, and dancing.

Many guests participated in the tradition to become an honorary Newfoundlander by puckering up their lips to smooch a cold fish.

Have you ever kissed a cod?

Six days after the first plane arrived,
a rainbow stretched over Gander as,
one by one, the planes left.

When the world was hurting
and hateful actions had
caused such sadness,
love and kindness had filled
the air in Gander.

In many ways, the world changed on September 11, 2001.

But during dark times, there are many who shine a light. The people of Gander were such a beacon.

The plane people flew in as strangers, and left as family.

Historical Note

Sometimes in the world, sad and scary events happen. On September 11, 2001, a terrible choice was made by some people to use airplanes to attack the World Trade Center buildings in New York City and the Pentagon in Washington, DC. This day is often referred to as 9/11. Many memorials have been created to remember the thousands of lives lost and people injured on that day. It was a frightening time for everyone around the world.

Communication looked a lot different in the year 2001. Cellphones existed, but not everyone had one. Most people used home phones. If you were away from home, there were phone booths with public pay phones to use. They were located in airports, in shopping malls, and on street corners. Cellphones did not take photos as they do now. You needed to carry a camera if you wanted photos or videos. Today we can see the news on our handheld devices, but back then, people learned about breaking news on the radio or television.

So when the tragic events of 9/11 happened, it caused a lot of confusion and fear.

In order to bring a stop to what was happening and prevent more airplane attacks, for the first time in history, all air travel was grounded in the United States. That meant every plane in the air that day had to land at the closest airport. Many of the pilots, crew members, and passengers on the planes did not know the reason they were being diverted (made to change directions) and forced to land. They were just told to follow the orders given.

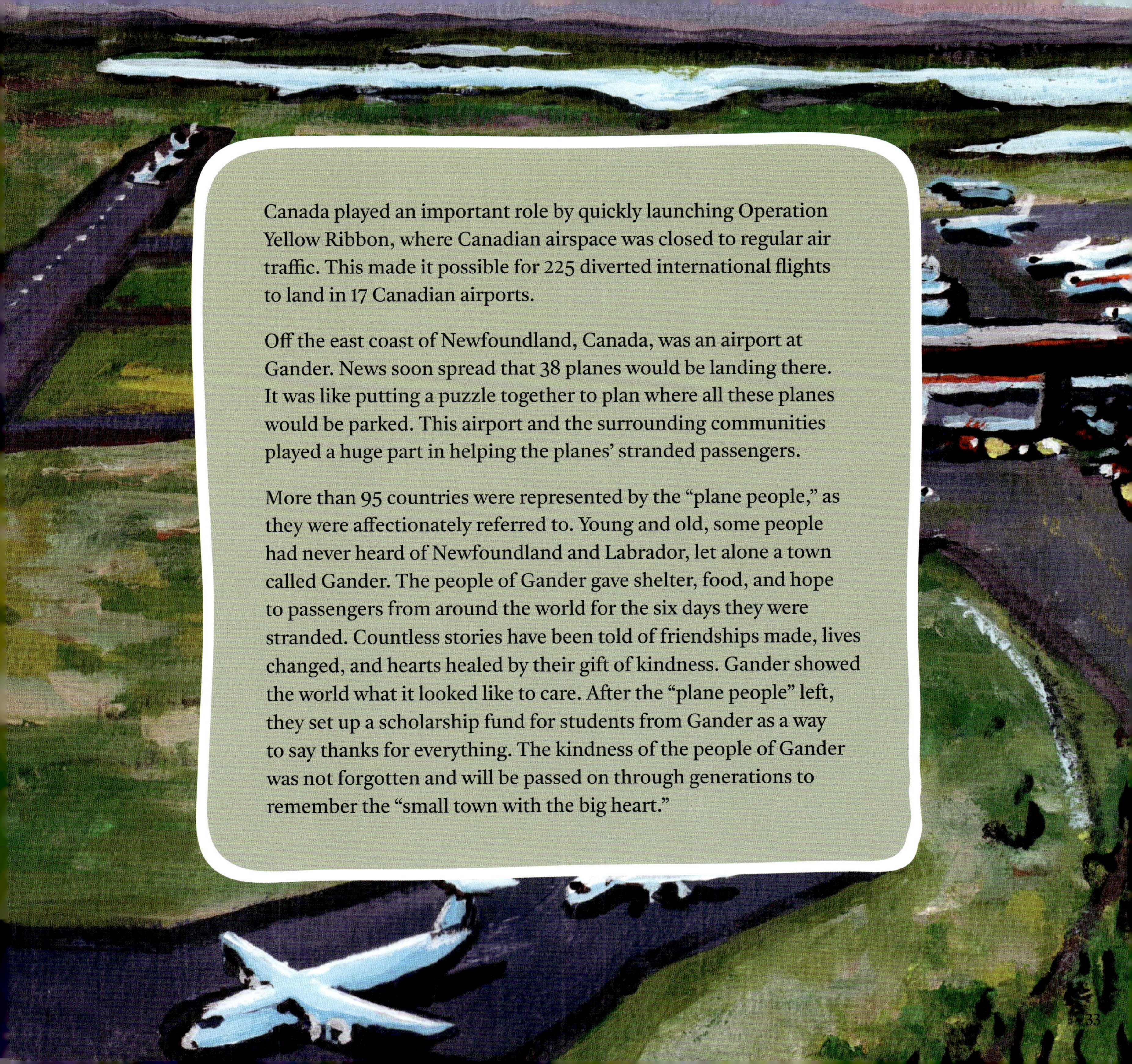

Canada played an important role by quickly launching Operation Yellow Ribbon, where Canadian airspace was closed to regular air traffic. This made it possible for 225 diverted international flights to land in 17 Canadian airports.

Off the east coast of Newfoundland, Canada, was an airport at Gander. News soon spread that 38 planes would be landing there. It was like putting a puzzle together to plan where all these planes would be parked. This airport and the surrounding communities played a huge part in helping the planes' stranded passengers.

More than 95 countries were represented by the "plane people," as they were affectionately referred to. Young and old, some people had never heard of Newfoundland and Labrador, let alone a town called Gander. The people of Gander gave shelter, food, and hope to passengers from around the world for the six days they were stranded. Countless stories have been told of friendships made, lives changed, and hearts healed by their gift of kindness. Gander showed the world what it looked like to care. After the "plane people" left, they set up a scholarship fund for students from Gander as a way to say thanks for everything. The kindness of the people of Gander was not forgotten and will be passed on through generations to remember the "small town with the big heart."

Did You Know?

- In 1938, the airport at Gander was known as Newfoundland Airport and had the largest airfield in the world at that time.
- During World War II, the airport was used for the movement of Allied aircraft, such as bombers, to Europe.
- After Newfoundland joined Canada in 1949, the airport was renamed Gander International Airport.
- By the 1950s, Gander International Airport was one of the busiest international airports in the world as flights had to stop to refuel before crossing the Atlantic. It became known as the "Crossroads of the World."
- On June 19, 1959, Queen Elizabeth II flew to Gander to open the new terminal building, which was one of the most modern in the world at the time.
- During the 1960s, the need for airports like Gander began to fade as newer jets could travel over long distances without having to stop for refuelling to cross the Atlantic.
- The *Come From Away* musical opened on Broadway in 2017 to tell the story of the passengers stranded in Gander on 9/11. A smash hit, it has been performed in theatres across Canada and the United States.
- One couple who met in Gander in September 2001 fell in love and were engaged two months later. They married in September 2002 and honeymooned in Newfoundland.
- Unga, one of the bonobos rescued from a plane stranded in Gander, went on to have an infant, and the zoo named her baby Gander.

Nikki Bergstresser, children's author, speaker, and educator, grew up in a small prairie town. Many of Nikki's books, such as *Seasons for Stones* and *A Promise to Protect*, share her love for community. Deeply moved by the true story of Gander, Newfoundland, she sees it as a reminder that in the hard moments, compassion and kindness can connect us. Nikki lives in Abbotsford, British Columbia, with her husband, two daughters, and a few mischievous furry critters. She loves plotting her next story while hiking in nature and makes new friends wherever she travels.

Reilly Fitzgerald grew up in Wabush, a small town in Newfoundland and Labrador, where his art skills were apparent early in life. Reilly, who is ambidextrous, completed a Fine Art program while in high school, and studied art and art history at Memorial University, earning a B.A. and a B.Ed. He has had a variety of jobs, including high school English teacher, art teacher, plasterer, and painter. Since 2011, Reilly has used his art as a therapeutic release from life-changing and debilitating chronic pain. Although he is mostly known as a fine artist, this is Reilly's second published children's book. Reilly lives with his high school sweetheart wife, Julie, in Clarenville. He creates his art at home and at his mother's cabin home in Denny's Pond, NL.

Library and Archives Canada Cataloguing in Publication

Title: Gander : the town that welcomed the world / by Nikki Bergstresser ; illustrated by Reilly Fitzgerald.
Names: Bergstresser, Nikki, author. | Fitzgerald, Reilly, illustrator.
Identifiers: Canadiana 20260160164 | ISBN 9781997872047 (hardcover)
Subjects: LCSH: September 11 Terrorist Attacks, 2001—Social aspects—Newfoundland and Labrador—Gander—Juvenile literature. | LCSH: Gander (N.L.)—History—21st century—Juvenile literature. | LCSH: Air travel—Newfoundland and Labrador—Gander—Juvenile literature. | LCSH: Aeronautics, Commercial—Newfoundland and Labrador—Gander—Passenger traffic—Juvenile literature. | LCGFT: Picture books.
Classification: LCC HV6432.7 .B47 2026 | DDC j973.931—dc23

Publisher Cataloguing-in-Publication Data (U.S.)

Names: Bergstresser, Nikki, author | Fitzgerald, Reilly, illustrator.
Title: Gander : the town that welcomed the world / by Nikki Bergstresser ; illustrated by Reilly Fitzgerald.
Description: First edition. | Oakville, Ontario : Plumleaf Press, 2026. | Summary: "On September 11, 2001, thousands of scared and confused travelers were stranded far from home in Gander, Newfoundland, where the community welcomed them with kindness, compassion, and East Coast heart"—Provided by publisher.
Identifiers: ISBN 978-1-99787-204-7 (hardcover)
Subjects: LCSH: September 11 Terrorist Attacks, 2001—Juvenile literature. | Gander (N.L.)—History—21st century—Juvenile literature. | Gander (N.L.)—Social life and customs—Juvenile literature. | Social action—Newfoundland and Labrador—Gander—Juvenile literature. | BISAC: JUVENILE NONFICTION / History / Canada / General. | JUVENILE NONFICTION / Social Topics / Kindness. | JUVENILE NONFICTION / Social Topics / Friendship. | JUVENILE NONFICTION / Volunteering.
Classification: LCC HV6432.B47 2026 | DDC 971.8 – dc23

Published in Canada by Plumleaf Press Inc. This is a first edition.

26 27 28 29 30 6 5 4 3 2 1

Original art created with acrylic paintings
Designed by Rebecca Bender, Aubryn Harvey

Plumleaf Press Inc.
100 Bronte Road, Unit 9, Oakville, ON, L6L 6L5
www.plumleafpress.com

Printed in China